TABLE OF CONTENTS

SUPPLIED BY:
ARGENT'S (Printed Music)
20 DENMARK STREET
LONDON WC2H 8NE
071-379 3384

For information concerning tapes of the songs in this book,
write to Ken Eldson, 2121 Linneman St., Glenview, Illinois 60025

©1980 BY MEL BAY PUBLICATIONS INC., PACIFIC, MO.
INTERNATIONAL COPYRIGHT SECURED. ALL RIGHTS RESERVED. PRINTED IN U.S.A.

Crawdad Song

Line 1:
You get a line and I'll get a pole,— hon-ey,—
G
5 5 5 5 5 2 5 5 2 0 5 5

Line 2:
You get a line and I'll get a pole,— babe,—
D7
2 5 5 5 5 0 5 5 2 5 5 0

Line 3:
You get a line and I'll get a pole, and we'll go down to the
G C
2 5 5 5 5 0 5 5 2 5 0 5 2 5 5

Line 4:
crawdad hole— hon-ey, sug-ar bab - y mine.—
G D7 G7
0 5 2 0 5 5 5 5 2 0 5 5

What you gonna do when the lake runs dry honey?
What you gonna do when the lake runs dry babe?
What you gonna do when the lake runs dry,
Sit on the bank and watch the crawdads die,
Honey, sugar baby mine.

Crawdad Song

Rye Whiskey

If the ocean was whiskey and I was a duck.
I'd dive to the bottom and never come up.

Way up on Clinch Mountain I wander alone,
I'm drunk as the devil, just leave me alone.

I eat when I'm hungry, I drink when I'm dry,
If a tree don't fall on me I'll live till I die.

Rye Whiskey

Banks of the Ohio

I asked my love___ to take a walk,___ just to walk___
D   A7

___ a lit-tle way,___ as we walk___ oh may we talk___
D   G

Chorus

all a-bout___ our wed-ding day.___ On-ly say___ that you'll be
D   A7   D   D

mine___ In my home___ we'll hap-py be,___ Down be-side___
A7   D

___ where the wa-ters flow, ___ on the banks___ of the O-hi-o.___
G   D   A7   D

Banks of the Ohio

The Roving Cowboy

Come all you rov-ing cow - boys, Bow down your souls by Land, —— I'll
Em

tell to you a stor - y, —— While you a - round me stand —— I'm

Goin' to quit this wild west, —— This bleak and storm - y plain: —— Where the

In - dians are I'll leave you to nev-er re - turn a - gain. ——

I've crossed the Rocky Mountains, I've crossed the Rocky Hills;
I've crossed the Rocky Mountains where many a brave boy's fell;
I've seen the distant country, The Indians and the Wild:
I'll never forget my old, old home, and mother's sweetest smile.

The Roving Cowboy

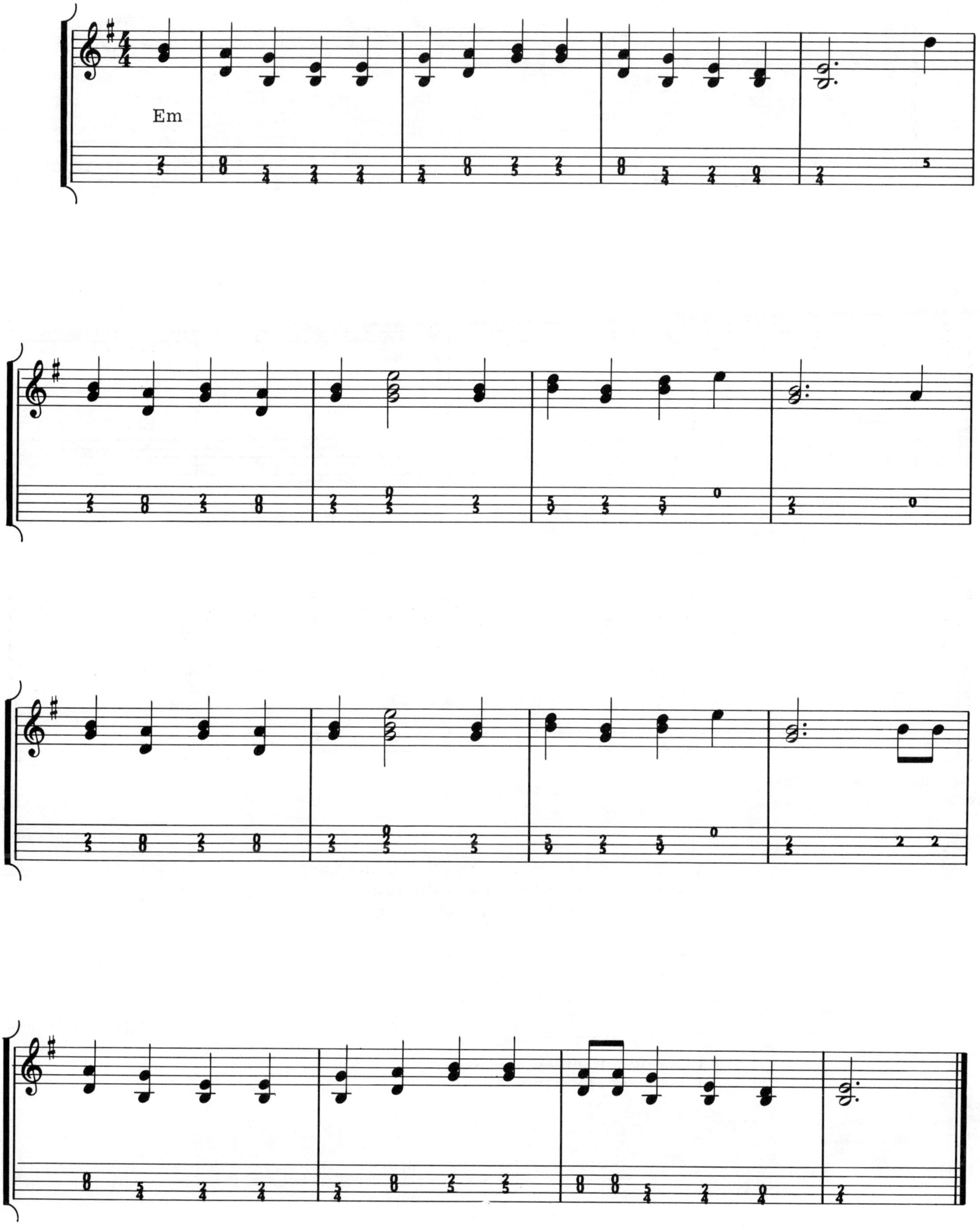

Red Rocking Chair

Ain't got no use for your red rock - ing chair._____ Ain't got no Sug-ar ba - by now_____

I ain't got no hon-ey ba - by now. _____

Who'll rock the cradle, who'll sing the song,
Who'll rock the cradle when I'm gone,
It's who'll rock the cradle when I'm gone.

I'll rock the cradle, I'll sing the song,
I'll rock the cradle when you're gone,
It's I'll rock the cradle when you're gone.

It's all I can do, It's all I can say,
I can't get along this-a-way,
I can't get along this-a-way.

Red Rocking Chair

Silent Night

Silent Night

Blow Away the Morning Dew

There was a far-mer's son,___ kept sheep u-pon a hill,___ And
G   D   G

he went out one May morn-ing to see what he could kill, Sing-ing
D   Em   C   D

blow a-way the morn-ing dew, the dew and the dew,___
G   C   G   C

Blow a-way the morn-ing dew, how sweet the winds do blow.___
G   Em   C   G   D   G

He looked high he looked low, he cast an under look,
And there he saw a fair pretty maid, a-bathing in the brook,
Singing, Blow away the morning dew...............

If you will come to my father's house which is walled all around,
Then you shall have your will of me and twenty thousand pound,
Singing, Blow away the morning dew..............

But when they came to her father's gate, so quickly she popped in,
And said, "There stands a fool without, and here's a maid within"
Singing, Blow away the morning dew...............

Blow Away the Morning Dew

Greenland Fishery

'Twas in eight - een hun - dred and fif - ty three And of
G   D7   G

June the thir - teenth day, ___ That our gal - lant ship her ___
Am   D7   G   Am

an - chor ___ weighed, And for Green - land bore ___ a -
D7   G   Am

way, brave boys, And for Green - land bore ___ a - way. ___
D   G   D7   G

The lookout in the crosstrees stood,
With his spy glass in his hand.
"There's a whale, there's a whale, there's a whalefish," he cried.
And she blows at every span, brave boys,
And she blows at every span."

Greenland Fishery

Bury Me Out on the Lone Prairie

Oh bu-ry me out on the lone prair - ie, ___

where the coy - otes howl ___ and the wind blows free ___

___ and when I die ___ you can bu - ry me ___

___ 'neath the West- ern sky ___ on the lone prair - ie ___

Bury Me Out on the Lone Prairie

The Drunken Sailor

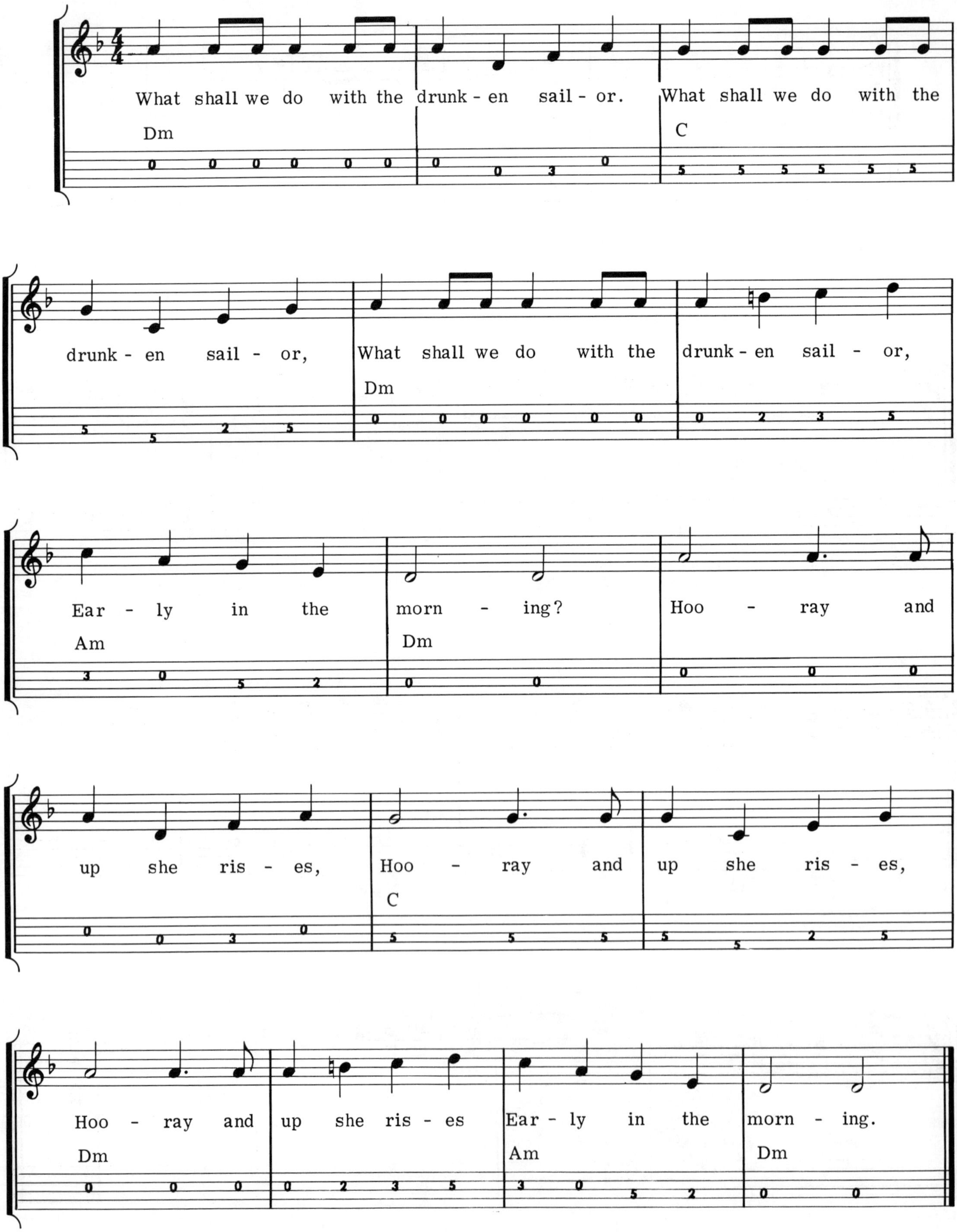

The Drunken Sailor

Knoxville Girl

I met a lit-tle girl in Knox - ville, a town you all know
D   D7   G

well,___ and ev - 'ry Sun - day eve - ning out in her home I'd
D   E7

dwell.___ We went to take an eve - ning walk a -
A7   D   D7

bout a mile from town.___ I picked a stick up
G   D

off of the ground and knocked that fair girl down.___
A7   D

Knoxville Girl

The Blue-Tail Fly

Slowly, ad lib

When I was young I used to wait on Mas-ter and fetch
G C D7

him his plate, and pass the bot-tle when he got dry, And
G C

Faster

brush a-way the blue-tail fly.
D7 G

Chorus

Jim-my Crack Corn, and
G

I don't care, Jim-my Crack Corn, and I don't care
D7 G

Jim-my Crack Corn, and I don't care, my mas-ter's gone a-way.
C D7 G

Blue - Tailed Fly

The Girl I Left Behind

I'm lone-some since I crossed the hill And o'er the moor and val - ley; Such heav-y thoughts my heart do fill since part-ing with my Sal - ly. I seek no more the fine and gay, For each but does re-mind me How swift the hours did pass a-way with the girl I left be-hind me.

Oh ne'er shall I forget the night,
The stars were bright above me,
And gently lent their silv'ry light
When first she vowed to love me.
But now I'm bound across the sea,
So heaven guide me kindly
And send me safely back again
To the girl I left behind me.

The Girl I Left Behind

The Big Rock Candy Mountain

On a sum - mer day in the month of May, a___ bur - ly bum came
G   D7   G   D7   G   D7

hik - ing   Down a sha - dy lane thru the sug - ar cane, he was
G   D7   G   D7

look - in for his lik - ing,   As he roamed a - long he
G   D7   G   D7

sang a song of the land of milk and hon - ey,   where a
G   D7 G   D7   G

bum can stay for___ man-y a day and he won't need an - y
D7   G   D7   G   D7

mon - ey.   Oh the buz-zin' of the bees in the cig - ar-ette trees, near the
G   G   G7

so - da wa - ter foun - tain, At the lem-on-ade springs where the
C   G   D7

blue - bird sings in the Big Rock Can - dy Moun - tain.
G   G   D7   G

The Big Rock Candy Mountain

The Ash Grove

Down yon - der green val - ley, where stream-lets me - an - der, when
F   Gm   G7   C

twi - light is fad - ing, I pen - sive - ly rove. or
F   Bb   F   C7   F

at the bright noon - tide in sol - i - tude wan - der, a -
Gm   G7   C

mid the dark shades of the lone - ly Ash Grove. 'Twas
F   Bb   F   C7   F

there while the black - bird was cheer - ful - ly sing - ing, I
F   D7   Gm   C7

Still glows that bright sunshine o'er valley and mountain,
Still warbles the blackbird his note from the tree;
Still trembles the moonbeam on streamlet and fountain,
But what are the beauties of nature to me?
With sorrow, deep sorrow, my bosom is laden,
All day I go mourning in search of my love,
Ye echoes! Oh tell me where is the sweet maiden?
"She sleeps 'neath the green turf down by the Ash Grove."

The Ash Grove

Home on the Range

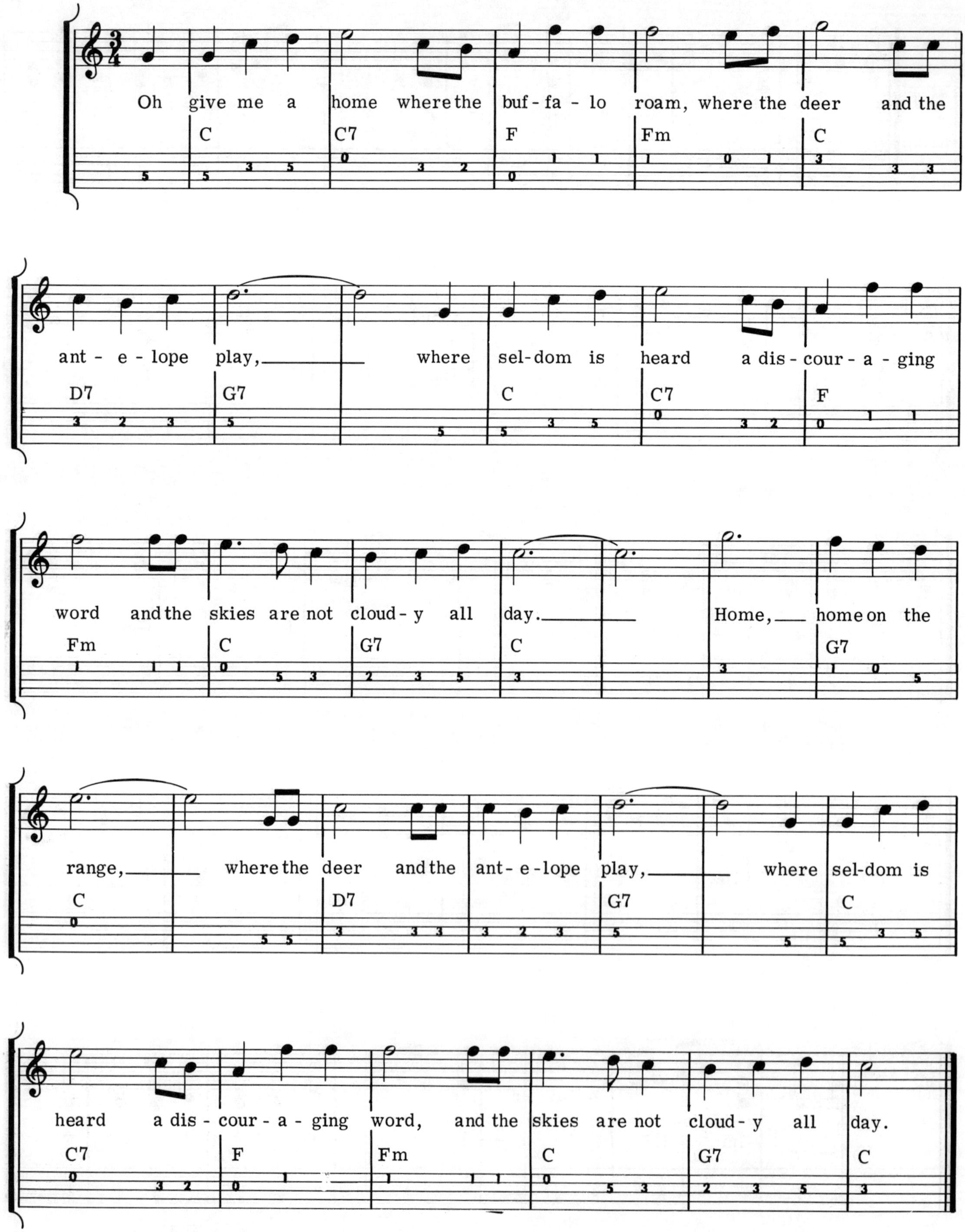

Home on the Range

Blow, Ye Winds

'Tis ad - ver -tised in Bos - ton, New - York and Buf-fa - lo, _____ Five

F   C7   F

hun - dred brave A - mer - i - cans, a - whal-ing for to go,   sing - ing

Gm   C7   F   Dm   G7   C7

Blow,   ye winds   in the morn - ing,   And blow   ye winds high -

F

o! _____ Clear a-way your run - ning gear, And blow ye winds High - O! _____

Bb   F   C7   F

Blow, Ye Winds

Sweet Betsy from Pike

Not too fast

Oh don't you re-mem-ber Sweet Bet-sy from Pike, who crossed the big moun-tains with

D   A7   D   E7

her lov-er Ike, with two yoke of cat-tle, a large yel-low dog, a___

A   Bm   F#m   G   D

tall Shanghai roost-er, and one spot-ted hog, say-ing "Good-bye Pike Coun-ty, Fare-

A7   D   **Chorus** D   A7

well for a-while, we'll come back a-gain when we're panned out our pile.

D   D   A7   D

The Shanghai ran off and their cattle all died;
That morning the last piece of bacon was fried;
Poor Ike was discouraged, and Betsy got mad,
The dog drooped his tail and looked wondrously sad.

Sweet Betsy from Pike

Down in the Valley

Down in the val - ley_____ val - ley so low,_____
G   D7

hang your head o - ver,_____ hear the wind blow_____
G

Hear the wind blow, _____ dear, _____ hear the wind blow_____
D7

hang your head o - ver_____ hear the wind blow_____
G

Build me a castle, forty feet high,
So I can see her as she goes by.
As she goes by dear, as she goes by,
So I can see her as she goes by.

Down in the Valley

Little Brown Jug

My wife and I live all a-lone in a lit-tle brown hut we call our own.
C F G7 C G7 C

She likes gin and I like rum. Lord-y but don't we have fun.
C F G7 C

Chorus

Ha ha ha you and me little brown jug don't I love thee
C F G7 C G7 C

Ha ha ha you and me little brown jug don't I love thee
C F G7 C

Little Brown Jug

Oh Suzanna

Oh I comefrom A - la - ba - ma with my ban - jo on my knee,___ I'm__
G D7

going to Lou - si - an - a my___ true love for to see.___ It rained so hard the
G D7 G

day I left, the weath-er it was dry,___ The__ sun so hot I froze to death, Su-
D7 G

zan - na don't you cry. ___ Oh Su - zan - na, oh don't you cry for
D7 G C G

me,___ for I comefrom A - la - ba - ma with my ban - jo on my knee__
D7 G D7 G

Oh Suzanna

Shenandoah

Oh Shenandoah, I love your daughter, Away, you rolling river,
Oh Shenandoah, I love your daughter.
Away, we're bound away, 'cross the wide Missouri.

Farewell my dear, I'm bound to leave you, away you rolling river,
Oh Shenandoah, I'll not deceive you.
Away, we're bound away, 'cross the wide Missouri.

Shenandoah

Turkey in the Straw

As__ I was a-goin' on | down the road with a | tired team and a
G

heav - y load, I | cracked my whip and the | lead - er sprung, I__
D7 | G

Chorus

says bye – bye to my | wag- on tongue. | Tur-key in the straw, | haw, haw, haw,
G D7 G | G

Tur-key in the hay | hay, hay, hay, | Roll 'em up and twist 'em up a
C | G

high tuck - a - haw And__ | hit 'em up a tune called | Tur-key in the Straw.
D7 | G | D7 G

Turkey in the Straw

There is a Tavern in the Town

There is _____ a tav - ern in the town, _____ in the
C

town, _____ and there _____ my dear love sits him down, _____ sits him
G7

down, _____ and _____ drinks his wine 'mid laugh - ter _____
C   C7   F

free, _____ and nev - er nev - er thinks of me. _____
G7   C

Chorus

Fare - thee well, for I must leave thee, do not let the part - ing
G7   C

grieve thee, and re - mem-ber that the best of friends must part, must

G7   C   F

part_____ A - dieu,_____ a - dieu kind friends a - dieu, a - dieu, a -

C   G7   C

dieu, _____ I can _____ no long - er stay with you, stay with

G7

you_____ I'll_____ hang my harp on a weep - ing wil - low

C   C7   F

tree,_____ and may_____ the world go well with thee._____

G7   C

There is a Tavern in the Town

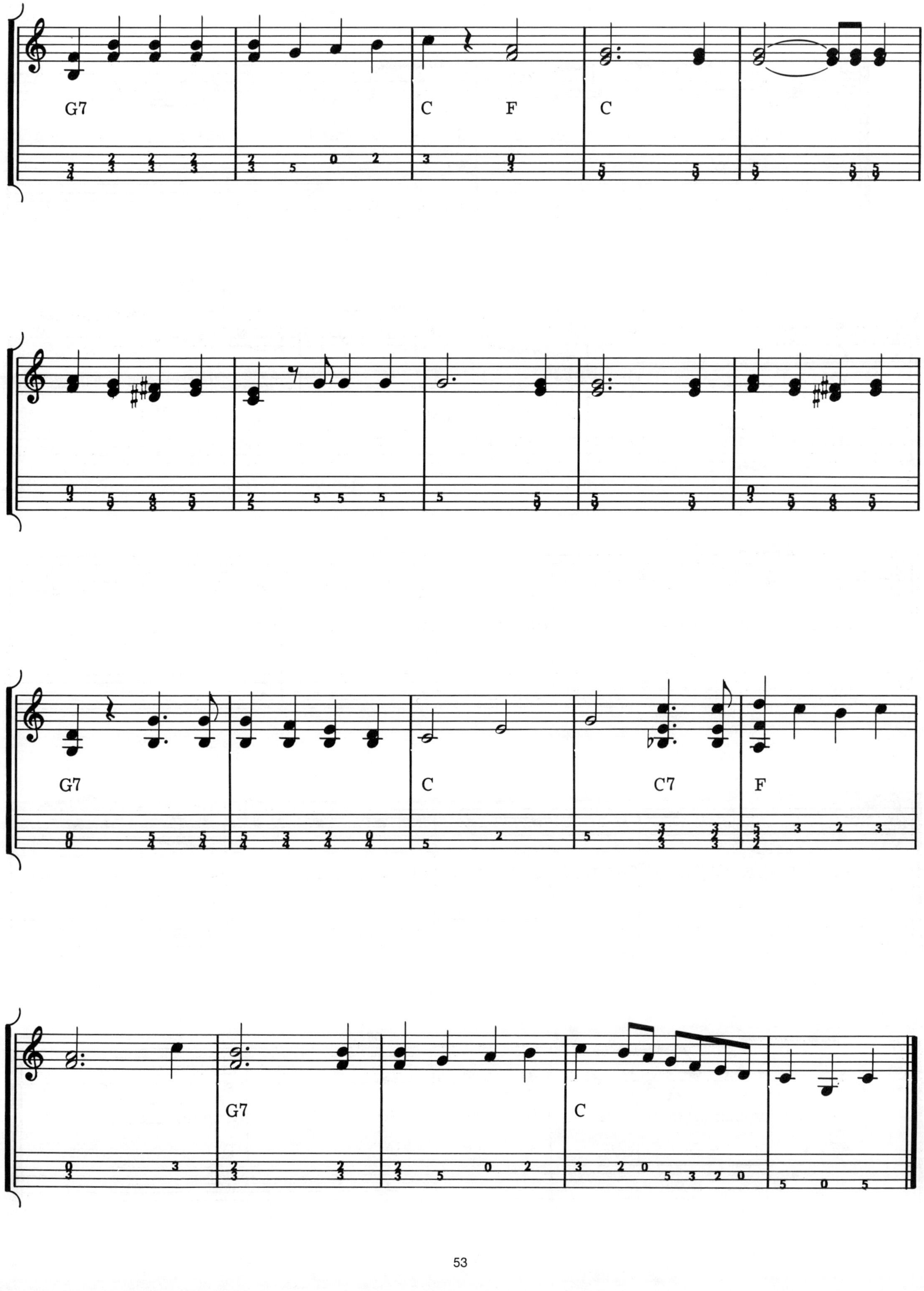
G7
C
F
C
G7
C
C7
F
G7
C

Rio Grande

Oh say was you ev - er in Ri - o Grande? 'Way,_____ you
D   A7   D

Ri - o!_____ Oh was___ you ev - er on___ that strand? For we're
G   D   A7   Bm

bound for the Ri - o Grande! And a - way_____ you
D   A7   D

Ri - o!_____ 'Way,_____ you Ri - o!_____ Sing fare you well, my
G   D

pret - ty young girls, for we're bound to the Ri - o Grande._____
A7   D   A7   D

Rio Grande

John Hardy

John Har - dy was a desperate lit - tle man,____ He carried two
guns ev - ery day.____ He killed him a man in the
West Vir - gin - ia land,____ you oughta see John Har-dy get-tin' a -way, Lord,
Lord,____ You oughta see John Har- dy get-tin' a - way.____

They took John Hardy to the hangin' ground,
They took him there to die,
The very last words that poor boy said,
"My forty-five never told a lie, Lord, Lord.
My forty-five never told a lie"

John Hardy

Red River Valley

From this val - ley they say you are go - ing____ We will miss your bright

C   F   C

eyes and sweet smile,____ For they say you are tak - ing the sun-shine____

G7   C   F

____ that bright-ened our path for a - while.____ Come and sit by my side if you

G7   C

love me____ Do not hast - en to bid me a - dieu,____ But re - mem - ber the

F   C   G7   C

Red River Val - ley____ and the cow - boy that loved you so true.____

F   G7   C

Red River Valley

Yankee Doodle

Yan - kee Doo - dle came to town a - rid - ing on a po - ny, He

C   G7   C   G7

3 3 5   0   3 0 5   3 3 5 0   3 2   5
                     5

stuck a feath - er   in his cap and   called it mac - a - ro - ni.

C   F   G7   C

3 3 5 0   1 0 5 3   2 0 2   3 3
                         5

Yan - kee Doo - dle   keep it up,   Yan - kee Doo - dle   Dan - dy

F   C

0 2 0 5   0 2 3   5 0 5 3   2 5

mind the mu - sic   and the step and   with the girls be   han - dy

F   C   G7   C

0 2 0 5   0 2 3 0 5   3 2 5   3 3

60

Yankee Doodle

Aloha Oe

Aloha Oe

Johnny Has Gone For a Soldier

1. Here I sit on But-ter milk Hill, who could blame me, cry my fill, and
ev-'ry tear would turn a mill John-ny has gone for a sol - dier.

2. Me oh my, I love him so, broke my heart to see him go, and
on-ly time will heal my woe, John-ny has gone for a sol - dier.

3. I'll sell my flax, I'll sell my reel,
   Buy my love a sword of steel,
   So it in battle he may wield,
   Johnny has gone for a soldier.

Johnny Has Gone For a Soldier

Goober Peas

Sit-ting by the road-side | on a sum-mer day, | Chat-ting with my mess-mates
C | F   C | C

pass-ing time a-way | Ly-ing in the shad-ow | un-der-neath the trees.
F   G | C | F

Good-ness how de-licious | eat-ing goo-ber peas | **Chorus** Peas! Peas! Peas! Peas!
C   F | C G C | C   F

Eat-ing goo-ber peas! | Good-ness how de-li-cious. | Eat-ing goo-ber peas!
G7   C | F | C G7 C

Just before the battle the general hears a row,
He says, "The Yanks are coming, I hear their rifles now,"
He turns around in wonder and what do you think he sees?
The Georgia Militia, eating Goober Peas! CHORUS

I think my song has lasted almost long enough.
The subject's interesting, but rhymes are mighty rough;
I wish this war was over, when free from rags and fleas,
We'd kiss our wives and sweethearts and gobble Goober Peas! CHORUS

Goober Peas

A-Roving

In Am-ster-dam there lived a maid, mark well what I do say!_____ In
D   A7   D   A7   D

Am-ster-dam there lived a maid And she was mis-tress of her trade, I'll
G   D   Em   E7   Bm   A7

go no more a - rov - ing with you fair maid!_____ A -
D   G   D   A7   D

rov - ing, a - rov - ing, Since rov - ing's been my ru - i - in I'll
G   D   Em   E7   Bm   A7

go no more a - rov - ing with you fair Maid!_____
D   G   D   A7   D

A-Roving

Chisholm Trail

Well come a-long boys and lis-ten to my tale, I'll
G

tell you of the trou-ble on the old Chis-holm trail, come-a ti - yi yip-pee, yip-pee
D7

yay, yip-pee yay, come-a ti - yi yip-pee yip-pee yay.
G   D7   G

I started up the trail October twenty-third,
I started up the trail with the two-u herd. CHORUS

No chaps, no slicker and it's pourin' down rain,
I swear, by gosh, I'll never night herd again. CHORUS

Chisholm Trail

Deep River

Slowly, with expression

Deep_____ Riv-er, my home is ov - er Jor-dan,___ Deep_____ Riv-er Lord, I

D Bm7   Em   G   D   Bm7   F#m   A7   D   D7   G   Em7

want to cross ov - er in - to camp-ground. Oh, don't you want__ to

D   Em   A7   D   Bm

go__ to that Gos - pel__ feast,__ that prom - ised Land__ where all__ is

F#m   Bm   G   F#m   A7   D   D7   G   Em   D   Em

peace?__ Deep_____ Riv- er, my home is ov - er Jor- dan,_____

F#m   A7   D   Bm7   Em   G   D   Bm7   F#m   A7

Deep_____ Riv - er Lord, I want to cross ov-er in - to Camp-ground.

D   D7   G   Em7   D   Em   A7   D

72